THE FIRST TRAVEL GUIDE TO THE MOON

RHODA BLUMBERG

THE FIRST TRAVEL GUIDE TO THE MOON

What to Pack, How to Go, and What to See When You Get There

Illustrated by Roy Doty

Four Winds Press

New York

LIBRARY OF CONGRESS CATALOGING IN PUBLICATION DATA
Blumberg, Rhoda.
  The first travel guide to the Moon.

  Bibliography: p.
  SUMMARY: A detailed travel guide outlining
travel arrangements, moon history, places of
interest, and other pertinent information for lunar
visitors.
  1. Space flight to the moon—Juvenile literature.
[1. Moon. 2. Space flight to the moon] I. Doty,
Roy, 1922— II. Title.
TL799.M6B55   919.9'104   [Fic]   80–66244
ISBN 0–590–07663–9

Published by Four Winds Press
A division of Scholastic Magazines, Inc., New York, N.Y. 10036
Text copyright © 1980 by Rhoda Blumberg
Illustrations copyright © 1980 by Roy Doty
All rights reserved
Printed in the United States of America
Library of Congress Catalog Card Number: 80–66244
1 2 3 4 5 84 83 82 81 80

I would like to thank David S. Rubin, of Croton-on-Hudson, New York, for his technical advice. I appreciate the time and interest given by Thomas Lesser, Senior Lecturer at the Hayden Planetarium of the American Museum of Natural History, and William O'Donnell, Chief of Media Services for NASA, who read the manuscript. They also guided me through Outer Space.

For my Space Cadets: Larry, Rena, Alice and Leda.

Contents

1

Plan Your Trip Now

It's never too early to start planning your vacation to the Moon. People all over the world have been signing up with their travel agents ever since regular flights started five years ago, in 1995. Reservations are in such demand that you must book your Moon trip months in advance.

The first tourist flight took place on October 12, 1992, five hundred years after Columbus discovered America.

To mark the Columbus Quincentennial Celebration, the space shuttle *Kirk One* lifted fifty passengers off the face of Earth. After a stopover at a space base satellite in the sky, the voyagers transferred to the *Lunar Trip*, a spaceship that landed them on the face of the Man in the Moon. The journey was so thrilling and the travelers were so enchanted by the wonders of a New World in outer space that grand tours were organized, and the Moon was developed as a holiday resort.

Our space shuttles leave from Vandenberg Earthport in California and from Kennedy Earthport in Florida. Tourists rocket away every two weeks. Consult timetables for the exact dates.

Foreign earthports offer excellent service, too. Europeans and Africans usually use the International Earthport in Kenya, and Asians head for the heavens from Sri Lanka's Celestial Center. These foreign earthports are built near the equator because the earth spins faster at the equator, so less fuel is needed for take-off. The foreign ports are newer, but not as large as the American earthports.

All shuttles land on Space Base, a satellite orbiting Earth. There passengers transfer to a Moon-bound ship. These shuttles return to Earth loaded with vacationers coming home from the Moon.

Ask your travel agent about Get-Away Specials. The

fare is cheaper when you join a group tour, pay student rates, or travel with your family.

There's a great vacation ahead, overhead, in a New World.

MAKING ARRANGEMENTS

Your travel agent works with the Lunar Tourist Bureau, a company with offices in most of the world's major cities. The Lunar Tourist Bureau (LTB) is licensed by the United Nations, which controls outer space. Note the quote from Article II of the 1967 "United Nations Treaty on the Principles Governing the Activities of States in the Exploration and Use of Outer Space Including the Moon and Other Celestial Bodies" —called the "Outer Space Treaty" for short:

> All activities on the Moon, including its exploration and use, shall be carried out in accordance with international law, in particular, the Charter of the United Nations.

Transportation, hotels, restaurants, businesses, sports centers, nature preserves, and settlements on the Moon are supervised by the United Nations Committee on the Peaceful Uses of Outer Space (UNCOPUOS), established 1961.

MONEY MATTERS

Your bank will change your currency into Moon money. Traveler's checks and major credit cards are accepted. Students can receive special discounts on most purchases.

HOW LONG SHOULD YOU STAY?

You can do everything in one day and one night, Moon time. That's four weeks Earth time. Moon days and nights are each two weeks long.

If you stay four weeks, you'll be able to see all the phases of Earth's waxing and waning in the sky. Earth goes through the same shapes the Moon does when we see it from Earth.

Plan to be away a month, or a "moonth," as they say up there.

WHEN SHOULD YOU GO?

Leave any time of the year. This is a vacation for all seasons. You don't have to worry about the weather, because the Moon doesn't have weather: no rain, fog, wind, or snow to spoil your fun. The forecast is always clear and cloudless.

Although the days are hot enough to boil water, nights are so cold that the Earth's North Pole is a hotspot by comparison. Still, you feel fine! When you're outside Moon-trekking, your space suit keeps out heat that can reach $+220°F$ ($105°C$) and cold that goes down to $-240°F$ ($-151°C$).

WHY GO TO THE MOON?

Reaching for the Moon used to mean trying for the impossible. The impossible dream has come true.

See the source of romance and poetry. Visit that Great Orange Ball in the Sky, the Queen of the Heavens, Ruler of Tides, Jewel of the Night.

The gorgeous scenery is different from anything you can find anywhere in the world. Mountains, craters, and canyons will have you starry-eyed—you'll feel as though you're part of the Milky Way. And when you've seen the blue light of Earth shining down from the sky above you, you'll never be the same. You will have new thoughts about life and your place in space.

It's good for the mind, and it's good for the body, too. The trip may be just what the doctor ordered. The Moon is germ-free. No shots are needed. What you breathe is always pure and unpolluted, whether it comes from your backpack or from air-conditioners. And there's less strain on your muscles, bones, and heart because your body isn't being pulled down by Earth's gravity.

Be a lightweight. During your journey to the Moon you are in zero gravity. That means there is no force to pull you down. Even if you're a three-hundred-pound

YOUR WEIGHT ON THE MOON	
EARTH	MOON
60 POUNDS	9.6 POUNDS
80 POUNDS	13.3 POUNDS
100 POUNDS	16.6 POUNDS
120 POUNDS	19.2 POUNDS
140 POUNDS	23.3 POUNDS

sumo wrestler you don't weigh anything. You are lighter than a hummingbird's feather and you float if you're not tied down.

Once you land on the Moon you are not weightless. The Moon does have gravity, but it's only one-sixth as strong as Earth's pull. You are able to keep your feet on the ground, but you feel light and bouncy.

Shake your worries away. With the first shimmy of your space shuttle you leave your Earthly troubles behind. What other vacation allows you to get away from it all? Lift your head above the clouds. Reach for the Moon.

2

What Should You Pack?

Leading sports shops and department stores sell government-approved space clothing and galaxy gear. Here is a list of necessary outfits:

CLOTHING

Coveralls for the journey. Buy lint-free nylon coveralls that have zipper pockets down the arms, across the chest, around the waist, and all over the pants. These pockets can be used for many items, such as pens, pads, minicalculators, wallets, photos, and good-luck charms. Coveralls should have elastic cuffs on the sleeves and legs so that they won't ride up in zero gravity. The latest model has sticky cloth on the pants seat. It helps keep you glued to your chair.

If you are not wearing coveralls you will not be allowed on board.

Astronaut suit for the outdoors. Although you can purchase an astronaut suit from a few select specialty shops, it's wiser to rent one after you've arrived on the Moon. You save money and packing space, and you have on-the-spot service. The Moon Rental Company with branches in all lunar hotels makes sure that your outfit fits properly. During your stay it cleans and repairs your suit and delivers it to your room within four hours.

The space suit is very comfortable. A special soft material protects you from harmful radiation and from the extremes of hot and cold. A light backpack of LOX (liquid oxygen) makes breathing easy. The suit comes with two pairs of elastic plastic underwear that hugs your body and puts pressure on your flesh. You need this ultrasnug underwear to live in outer space. Don't forget to wear it, or you'll explode.

A helmet which screws on to your collar has a visor designed to protect your eyes against the burning brilliance of the sun. Remember, there's no atmosphere to shield you from its glare and radiation. A two-way radio inside the helmet enables you to carry on conversations. Sound doesn't travel on the airless Moon. Therefore, even if you screamed no one would hear you. Your voice must be radioed to another person's tuned-in headset.

Pick out a helmet with a scratch-patch inside. If your

nose itches, you can turn your head and rub it against a piece of rough cloth. It's a small item, a bit expensive, but it can stop an itch or a twitch.

Special padded gloves and shoes complete your outfit. You'll be able to pick up and step on the hottest and coldest rocks.

The astronaut suit was designed by NASA engineers. What a contrast to the old twentieth-century space suit that weighed thirty-three pounds and had twenty-one layers of fabric. It was difficult to bend down and get around when wearing it. Compare your suit with the one used by Neil Armstrong. It's like comparing a skin-diver's suit with an ancient diving bell, or a football uniform with a medieval suit of armor.

Leisure clothing. Moon hotels are very informal. Men don't wear ties or jackets; women have no need for long, fancy dresses. Pack a few light, wipe-clean outfits. The Moon's water supply is limited, and all clothing is cleaned with chemically saturated pads.

Don't overpack! Each tourist is allowed forty-four pounds (twenty kilos) Earth weight. That's about seven pounds of Moon weight. No exceptions. Spaceships do not divide travelers into First Class and Coach. The same rules apply to everyone.

HANDY ITEMS TO TAKE WITH YOU

TV telephone. Your pocket-size computer TV telephone connects with any phone on Earth. This marvelous instrument allows you to see and talk with your family and friends back home. You can call people on the Moon, too, thanks to the Lunar Central System.

Camera. Even if you're not an expert shutterbug, your pictures will be clear, because there's no air or mist on the Moon. The best model for outer space is the Mini-Moonamatic. You can also buy an excellent Mini-Moonamatic Movie Camera.

Lingo translator. Here's another pocket-size computer. It translates conversations into twenty-three different languages. You'll enjoy using it when you meet tourists, whether they come from India, Scandinavia, Bolivia, or Zambia.

Beacon belt. This important safety device flashes red when you stray from your group. It turns green when you head back in the right direction.

Luna watch or clock. You'll want to know the date and time of your home on Earth, as well as the time on the Moon. The Luna Tick Watch Company produces the best timepieces.

Magnetic games. Cards, checkers, backgammon, Scrabble, Monopoly, and Star Wars games have been specially designed for Moon travelers. The pieces have magnets to anchor them down. You'll enjoy these games in Moon gravity and in zero gravity.

Don't forget anything. Home is a quarter of a million miles away.

3

All Aboard!

Check in at a hotel near the Earthport the night before your flight. You need a good night's rest before you're outward bound.

Wake-up time is 5:30 A.M. After breakfast at the coffee shop, a bus takes you to your Earthport. You should arrive at least an hour before blast-off, which is usually at 8:00 A.M. (weather permitting).

After you hand in your ticket, your luggage is weighed and sent separately to your space shuttle. A small bus takes you to the launch pad, where an outside elevator lifts you thirty stories to the top of the rocket ship. After crossing a short bridge, you climb down a ladder into the shuttle. A flight attendant helps you find your seat.

The latest-model shuttle carries seventy tourists. The crew consists of the pilot, a copilot, a flight engineer, and five attendants. The shuttle, a double-winged craft with three engines, goes back and forth between an Earthport and Space Base. Two huge rockets are attached to the ship, one on each side. The shuttle rides piggyback on an enormous fuel tank.

Place your hand luggage in the zipper pocket under your contour chair. Then fasten your safety belts—all of them: ankle strap, thigh strap, waist strap, shoulder strap. They prevent you from floating around. Eyeglasses must be strapped around your head to keep them from floating. You feel as though you're wearing a straitjacket, but you must buckle down to fly right! An attendant comes by to make sure all safety belts are buckled.

You must remain in your seat at all times during the short shuttle trip. Don't fidget. It usually takes about one hour before you are anchored at Space Base, where you transfer to the plane that goes to the Moon.

LIFT-OFF

Ready for take off? The control tower broadcasts the countdown over the ship's loudspeakers.

Brace yourself at number 10. At number 3 you hear noise that sounds as though you're sitting underneath Niagara Falls. The ship shudders and shakes.

At zero it's up and away. You roar into space, as you watch the takeoff on the small TV screen in front of your seat. You're riding on huge flames, rocketing away.

After a few minutes, when you're up twenty-five

miles, you feel a jolt. If you look outside you'll see the two large rockets dropping off the ship. The plane seems to be falling apart!

Don't panic. During every flight the pilot releases these rockets which descend by parachute into the ocean. They are picked up by Earthport ships, hauled in, fixed up, and used again for other shuttle flights.

Shortly after the rockets are released you'll feel another thud. Although you seem to be floating, your heart may be sinking when you see the fuel tank fall off, and there's sudden silence. The motors have stopped.

Relax. The tank is being dumped because all the fuel has been used up. There's no need for fuel as the ship starts orbiting Earth.

Look outside. You'll see with your own eyes: the Earth is round.

Although the sun is brighter than you ever saw it, the sky is jet black. (You won't see a blue sky again until you return to the atmosphere, the blanket of air that surrounds our globe.) Stars shine everywhere.

Of course, your nose is pressed against your window as

you start circling planet Earth at 17,500 miles per hour
If you're lucky you may see China's Great Wall.

Before you complete one orbit of the Earth, the pilot
uses small rockets to steer the shuttle to Space Base, three
hundred miles above earth.

DOCKING AT SPACE BASE

It takes about ten minutes for your ship to hook onto
Space Base, the human-made satellite used as a way
station to the Moon. You feel a bump when the shuttle
locks into its dock. A circular ring on the shuttle fits a
sealing ring on the harbor. Magnetic clamps grip the
ship, and steel claws lock into each other.

Outside your window you see dockworkers in space
suits guiding your shuttle to a perfect landing. The
workers are tethered to Space Base by long lifelines.
These lines keep them from drifting away and going into
orbit forever after.

When the shuttle is safely moored, green lights flash
above your seat. Wait until the pilot announces that it's
time to unbuckle.

Grab handrails along the walls of the ship, or use the
guide ropes stretched along the aisles. You must hold on

to something or you will float. Don't hurry, and don't push. Pull yourself to the open hatch. Then, holding guide ropes, "walk" with your hands through a short tunnel into port.

SPACE BASE

Space Base, three hundred miles above Earth, is the stopover for lunar tourists. Supply ships headed for the Moon stop here, too. Stevedores carry bulky but weightless cargo that comes up from Earth in unmanned robot ships. They transfer the freight into large containers which are then shot by giant cannons to a supply depot on the Moon.

You wait for your Moonliner in a room called Windows of the World. The room is a semicircle of glass with window seats for everyone. Once again, you must be strapped in so that you don't float around, for you are still in zero gravity. Chairs are on the floor and the ceiling. Reserve an "upper." You won't feel odd hanging with your head down because there's no gravity to pull blood to your head. And although you don't feel topsy-turvy, the experience is offbeat.

You relax at Space Base for one and a half hours, the time it takes the base to orbit Earth once.

Around the world in ninety-three minutes! It takes only ten minutes to cross the United States, and twenty-five to fly over the Pacific Ocean. Because orbits don't always go the same route, you never know what you'll see.

A telescope in front of each seat has attachments for your camera. You may be able to zoom in on Egypt's pyramids, Russia's Kremlin, or India's Taj Mahal. Use color film. The Sahara and Gobi deserts show up in vivid reds, golds, oranges, and browns. Oceans are swirls of greens and blues. Icebergs and polar caps are a dazzling blue-white. When orbiting you see both day and night. Earth at night shows forest fires, lightning streaks, and city lights that sparkle like jewels. Keep clicking your camera. If Earth isn't socked in by pollution or by clouds, you'll have marvelous photos to show the folks back home.

Although Lunar Trip officials prefer that you remain seated during most of your stay at Space Base, you can leave your chair to float around, climb the walls, and walk along the ceiling. There are lots of tricks you can try in zero gravity, but be patient. You'll have plenty of time to amuse yourself during your two-day journey to the Moon.

4

Heading for the Moon

A voice over the loudspeaker lets you know when it's time to board your Moonliner. Attendants show you the ropes. You use them to pull yourself hand over hand to Moonship. No need to shake a leg. Your hands do the walking. You float on air, and you move in slow motion. A spacey, lunar dream is real!

MOONLINER

Because there's no gravity to hold it back and no air to slow its speed, Moonliner doesn't need a huge fuel tank. Small rockets launch it on its way to the Moon.

As soon as you enter Moonliner, sit down, buckle up, and batten down the way you did in the shuttle. A jolt sets you back in your seat during takeoff. After that you don't feel as though you're moving. It's smooth sailing to the New World.

You're allowed to get up and float around. Note the sign "Keep off the ceiling." The crew stores equipment there. Because you have no sense of up and down, the ceiling is colored orange, and the floor is brown. Use the handles and straps along the wall to pull yourself around and to stop when you want to stay in one place.

You're a changed person during your Moon journey, and you look like one, too. You have a swelled head, a red face, and your legs are skinnier than usual. That's because, without gravity, there's more blood in your head and less in your feet. Your coveralls are loose, and they are short because you're an inch or two taller. In weightlessness you stretch out due to more fluid in your spine.

Moonliner is equipped to take care of your eating, sleeping, washing, and exercising during your two-day voyage.

MEALS ON BOARD

You are served a big gala dinner shortly after Moonliner's takeoff. The food is delicious and the service, superb. Attendants hover over you like angels.

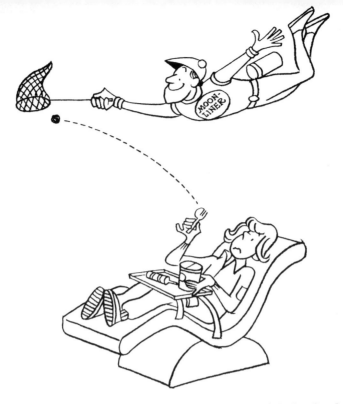

Buckle your thigh straps so that you don't kick the food tray clamped over your lap. Magnets hold sporks (a combination spoon and fork) and cans of food. The cans have plastic covers designed to keep food from escaping even when a spork dips into them.

Eating in outer space takes know-how. Push the spork through a plastic cover. If you don't aim carefully when you take the food out and bring it toward your mouth, you could end up with egg on your face or mashed potatoes in your hair. Keep your mouth wide open, and shut it fast once the food is past your teeth. The best technique is a smooth, archlike motion, tipping the spork into your mouth slowly.

It's not unusual to see spaghetti, a prune, or a meatball floating around. Flight attendants are very understanding. They swoop up stray foods, netting them as they flit around overhead.

Drinks come in plastic squeeze tubes. Puncture the tip with your teeth and sip carefully. Should liquid escape it forms perfectly shaped balls that drift in the ship's air. They're beautiful—especially the purple ones made from grape juice. But they must be chased and bagged by a busy crew.

WASHING UP

What a relief to see how well the washroom is designed! A vacuum inside the toilet acts as a substitute for gravity. Instead of a sink you use wash-and-wipe paper cloths which are pasted to the walls. No hair combing, beard brushing, moustache clipping, or shaving is permitted. Who needs floating hairs in the air?

For a time the lunar liners tried brushes and razors with vacuum-bag attachments, but there were too many leaks. For the past year these gadgets haven't been in the washrooms. (We can fly to the Moon, but we can't make a vacuum hairbrush that works!)

SLEEPING ACCOMMODATIONS

Although you could sleep floating in the air, this is against the rules. You sleep standing up in a sleeping bag that hangs on the wall near your seat. When you are tired, just stand against the wall, wrap the canvas around you, and zip yourself in. Be sure to place the bonnet part over your head or you'll feel so scatterbrained you won't be able to sleep.

Lullaby music is piped into your bonnet. There's a turn-off/tune-out switch for those who don't want sandman melodies.

When you unzip your sleeping bag, you float out like a genie coming out of a bottle.

EXERCISING

Because muscles start to go soft as soon as you leave Earth's gravity, one of the crew conducts easy exercises every four hours. For example, you do head nods, knee and arm bends, and flutter kicks. You frown, grin, grit your teeth, and wiggle your toes in rhythms set by the maestro muscle builder. You're bound to laugh about it. That's fine! Laughing is good for the cheeks and chest.

Use the exercise machines located in the back of the ship. Strap yourself to the seat of a stationary bike. Lock your feet in the stirrup pedals and ride the skies.

Are you a jogger? Head for the treadmill. A waist belt attached to the wall keeps you in place as your feet touch a slippery surface. You feel as though someone's holding you up while you're jogging.

Have you ever dreamed that you were a circus acrobat? Sign up on the attendant's schedule sheet for time in the Flash Gordon Padded Room, located behind the bike. Only six passengers are allowed in at a time. You can do midair somersaults, fly, walk the walls, and dance on the ceiling. Stand on someone's shoulders. Break away—you'll be suspended in midair. Perform a headstand

while someone using one finger holds you up. You're Wonder Woman, you're Spider Man, you're Mighty Mouse!

MOVIES AND TELEVISION

Each seat has its own screen. You can tune in to your favorite TV station or dial a movie, lecture, or concert. And you can always phone home, using your pocket TV phone.

THE SHOW OUTSIDE

You're never, never bored. Most of the time you are glued to your window, watching the world go by. You circle the Moon during the last hours of the journey. The sight of the mountains and craters are so fabulous that you won't need any other entertainment.

5

The Moon, at Last!

Moonliner lands gently in the middle of Clavius Crater. Unfasten your safety harnesses. You no longer float, because the Moon has gravity. It's six times weaker than Earth's gravity, and, therefore, you feel six times lighter than you did at home.

Divide your weight by about six. If you tip the scales back home at two hundred pounds, you weigh 33.3 pounds on the Moon. No crash diets needed to feel slim, svelte, and springy. (See page 7.)

Once Moonliner has landed and taxied to its moorings, it's down the hatch, through a tunnel, and into the large, underground Moon Central Station. Here escorts are waiting to lead you to minibuses which ride through underground shopping arcades connecting Moon Central Station with all hotels. You'll have plenty of time to shop here during your holiday.

Check into your room as soon as possible. You must rest and give your mind and body time to become adjusted to a new world.

HOTELS

You have a choice of four hotels, each rated from one to five stars. The number of stars, awarded by the Lunar Tourist Bureau, is based upon comfort, service, and luxury.

The *Zodiac* (★) attracts astrology and astronomy conventions. *Honeymoon Haven* (★★★★) gets the carefree rocket set, formerly called the jet set. The *Milky Way Lodge* (★★) attracts a family crowd and caters to school groups on class trips. *Crescent Earth Inn* (★★★) is the most popular and the oldest of the tourist resorts.

Although built and managed by Americans, Chinese, and Russians, who were the Moon's first immigrants, the

hotels are not owned by any nation or private company. Article XI of the United Nations Outer Space Treaty states:

> . . . neither the surface nor the subsurface of the Moon shall become the property of any State.

Hotels are underground. The rocky crust of the Moon is excellent protection against harmful radiation and against the extreme temperatures of hot and cold. All rooms are pressurized and air-conditioned. Although the Moon has been pocked by meteorites, the chances of being hit by one are about as small as the chance of being struck by lightning on Earth. You're as safe as you'd be in your own home.

Bedrooms are comfortable. No worries about lumpy mattresses, because there aren't any. You sleep on a plastic platform that feels as soft as a cushion because your body doesn't press down the way it does in Earth's gravity. Elastic plastic sheets are snapped around the bed. They hug you and make you feel a bit heavier and less spacey. All furniture is plastic, metal, glass, or ceramic. There aren't any Moon forests, so don't expect to knock on wood. Closet shelves go to the ceiling. You can reach the top with a hop. The ceiling is padded, in case you jump too high.

There is color television in every room, offering a variety of entertainment. Tune in to a local lunar station, or turn the dial to your favorite program back home. The SBC (Satellite Broadcasting Company) brings you TV broadcasts from Moscow, Madrid, Montreal, Paris, Peking, Peoria, and hundreds of other places around the globe.

Be sure to read the notices posted in every room: "In case of emergency, oxygen masks will be released from the ceiling. You will receive instructions by loudspeaker." All announcements are in Arabic, Chinese, English, French, Russian, and Spanish—the official languages of the United Nations. Translating computers installed in the walls change messages into forty-seven additional languages. You'll know what's going on whether you come from Burma or Bulgaria. Just press the button next to your country's flag, put on the attached earphones, and listen carefully.

Even though hotels are from two to four stories tall, there aren't any elevators. Ramps lead from floor to floor. In addition, halls have poles like those in firehouses. Just

hoist yourself up. You only weigh as much as an earthling infant. Slide down. You slip slowly.

NEWSPAPERS

The *Daily Planet* and the *Morning Moon* are at newstands in your hotel lobby.

Pick up a free copy of "This Week on the Moon," which is usually stacked at the front desk. It lists entertainment and special events.

ENTERTAINMENT

The huge underground Astro Center has theaters, sports arenas, and gymnasiums.

Visiting actors present the best Broadway and London hits. Ballet companies are star attractions. Dancers delight in leaps, twirls, and midair spins that are superhuman by Earth's standards. Toe dancers don't need slippers; they dance barefoot. (You, too, can dance on tiptoe due to weak gravity.)

Dancers perform to taped music. Because different muscle power and pressure are necessary, the usual instruments are not tuned for heavenly harmonies. New instruments are being designed. Until they are perfected all lunar symphony concerts are televised from Earth, by satellite.

Every once in a blue Earth a troop of acrobats who call themselves "The Astrobats" visits outer space. Don't miss them! They perform trapeze acts over the audience's heads, clowning as they throw each other from one end of the room to the other.

LOUNGES

All hotels have ramps to Pleasure Domes, above

ground glass-domed observation lounges made with a special type of glass that has been mined on the Moon. The glass is perfect protection against the outside, and it's tinted to shield your eyes against the fierce rays of the searing sun. (Moon glass is becoming easier and cheaper to mine and mold. A hotel on the drawingboards will be an aboveground glass structure. It's to be called the *Star Scraper*, and it will probably be the first deluxe five-star hotel.)

Some of your finest hours will be spent in the Pleasure Dome Lunar Lounges. You will see more stars than you ever saw in your life. They shine twenty times brighter than they do when seen from Earth, and they don't twinkle because there's no air to make them shimmer and blink.

Earth shines in the sky above, a beautiful blue ball that appears four times bigger and eighty times brighter than your at-home Moon. It has phases exactly like the Moon's. How romantic it is to see crescent Earth! What poetry and music have been inspired by half Earth! Full Earth, always seen in the Moon's midnight sky, is mind-boggling. (Some people insist it can cause insanity, but this is merely a superstition.)

6

Sports

THE ASTRO SPORTS CENTER

Rent wings and fly in the Astro Center's Luke Skywalker Room. The wings slip over your arms and tie around your thighs. A series of five lessons is included in the rental cost. You learn how to take off and "brake" for a soft landing. Should you sign up for the advanced figure-flying classes, instructors teach loops, swoops, and figure eights. Class A students play midair touch football (no flying tackles allowed).

The Lunatrick Gym is a *must*, because you have to

keep your muscle tone. You can exercise to your heart's content, because heart muscles don't have to work so hard on the Moon.

Want to "pump iron"? Try weight lifting. A six-hundred-pound barbell weighs about one hundred pounds on the Moon.

Enjoy acrobatics. You leap through the air with the greatest of ease. When you jump, the floor feels like a trampoline. Many people do spins and back flips as expertly as circus performers.

There is an outdoor volleyball court, but there's no baseball or football, because a good throw could easily go half a mile—right out of the ball park.

There's also a bowling alley. Balls are made from Moonrocks.

Good news, swim fans. The Big Dipper, an Olympic-size swimming pool, has just opened. Because there isn't a drop of natural water on the Moon, you swim in water made in a chemical laboratory.

The Apollo 14 Golf Driving Range is outside, above the Astro Center. Astronaut Alan Shepard started the sport in 1971, when he brought a golf ball with him and teed off on the Moon. His drive was out of sight. Of course, you wear your space suit. Be sure your swing doesn't lift you so high that you sweep yourself off your feet. Some golfers put weights in their shoes.

How about a game of basketball in the Astro Center basketball court? The baskets are thirty feet above the floor—an easy hop for a good player.

The best, most fantastic exercise is trekking around the Moon.

LUNAR TREKKING

Don your space suit and your LOX pack. Ready for adventure? Before you leave, ask the doorman to check you for leaks. Your blood could boil or turn to ice if you're not sealed into your clothes when you're outside. And LOX means life and breath, so be sure your pipes aren't clogged.

The Lunar Tourist Bureau arranges mountain-climbing and crater expeditions. They're called "Space Safaris." Climbing Moon mountains and exploring crannies and craters are experiences worth writing home about. You cover lots of ground. You don't walk; you lope like a kangaroo. Each step measures at least ten feet. You feel as though you're wearing seven-league boots.

Warning: Don't hop too far. Before you realize it, you could be lost. You should wear a beacon belt: it flashes red if you are off the hotel beam, and green if you're heading in the right direction. Beacon belts can be adjusted to aim at buddies, buses, and tour leaders, too.

TIPS FOR ROCK COLLECTORS

Pick up all the rocks you want, then sort them out when you're in your hotel room. A copy of "The Moonraker's Guide to Rocks" will help you identify your finds. You can pack only a few choice specimens. Remember that your travel weight is limited.

Look for "moon mirrors": glass that sticks on rocks and is mixed in soil. Natural glass is rare on Earth, but up here it's very common. Small, colorful glass beads found in the soil look great set in rings and bracelets. And stones with glass swirling through them make attractive paper-weights.

How about owning a chunk of the Moon's "green cheese"? That's what green rocks are called. They are collectors' items. You may be lucky enough to find rocks flecked with gold and silver. Serious treasure hunters look for odd-shaped crystals that can't be found on Earth.

Shops in the arcade sell Moon stones at sky-high prices. Pick your own, and save.

BIKING

It's a cinch to pedal uphill, and it's possible to ride at one hundred fifty miles per hour, but it's foolhardy to go that fast. You could fall into a minicrater. Always go bicycling with a buddy and stay near the hotel area, where crannies and craters are fenced off.

WAN HOOING

About five hundred years ago, the Chinese mandarin Wan Hoo invented a flying chair. Holding a kite in each hand, servants lit forty-seven rockets fastened to his chair-plane. Wan Hoo flew! He had hoped to reach the Moon. He never arrived, although he may have reached Heaven.

Flying chairs are called "Wan Hoos" in honor of his daring and imagination. The arms of the chair have push-button controls. The chair is fueled with nitrogen gas carried in a backpack. It is like the flying chair which was tried in Skylab in 1973 and 1974.

BELT AND SHOE FLYING

Strap a rocket belt to your waist, and fly like Superman. Boots called shoe flyers help you steer your course.

You wiggle your toes to press buttons that set off minirockets. The boots allow your arms to be free while you trip the light fantastic. (Skylab astronauts experimented with the first shoe flyers.)

Wan Hooing and rocket-belt flying are great sports, but they're not intended for sight-seeing. There are better means of transportation.

MOON BUGGIES

Also called Moonmobiles, they are open trucks that seat six—the driver-guide and five tourists. Frequent stops enable passengers to leave the buggy and leap about.

SPACE PLANES

These "flying hotels" are equipped with kitchens, and sleeping bags for twelve passengers. Some space-plane excursions last six (Earth) days.

Pick up a space-plane timetable, and book your seat at least three days in advance.

You'll want to see most of the Moon. That's a lot of sight-seeing, because this Heavenly Body has an area about four times that of the United States.

7

Transportation

MOON BUSES

Each bus has an enclosed "Earth" environment
enough oxygen to supply a dozen passengers fo
hours—even though the longest bus excursion las
hours, or five Earth days. A well-equipped galle
comfortable bunk beds make touring a pleasure.
have large windows and glass tops that are ide
sight-seeing. They are built to climb up and dow
sides of hills without overturning. Don't worry ab
flat tire. Tires are metal, because rubber would m

8

Excursions

TRIP #1. CIRCLE TOUR OF THE EASTERN SEAS

Sign up for this tour. You explore five seas, two lakes, and one marsh.

Planes shuttle back and forth between Moon Central Station and the Sea of Tranquility Spaceport. Your Circle Tour starts and ends at Tranquility. (For your reference, there is a map on page 57.)

Be sure you buy a round-trip ticket on the *Seafarer* spaceplane. It makes local stops allowing you time to explore all these places. You won't get your feet wet because all seas, oceans, bays, marshes, lakes, and lagoons on the Moon are dryer than dust. They were named by astronomers who thought they saw heavenly bodies of water when they looked through their telescopes.

The highlight of this trip is the visit to Tranquility Base, which you see either before or after you have circled the Eastern Seas.

TRANQUILITY BASE

Buggies take tourists to the historic landing place of Neil Armstrong and Buzz Aldrin, the first men on the Moon. Their spaceship, *Eagle*, came down on the west bank of the Sea of Tranquility thirty-one years ago, on July 20, 1969.

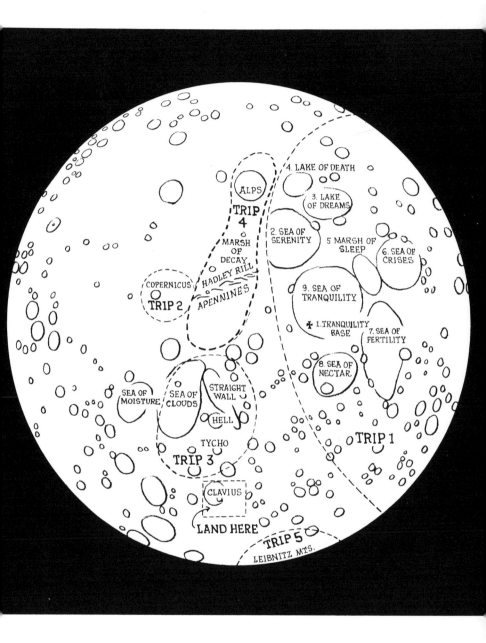

THE NEAR SIDE

You stand behind ropes to see their TV camera still on its tripod, two of their backpacks, and some overshoes left behind. A nylon American flag that they planted has waves and billows bent into it so that it seems to fly in this windless world.

You also see the astronauts' footprints, which are as fresh as the day they were made. These footprints won't disappear for millions of years because there's no wind or rain to erase them—and because you're not allowed to walk over them. It takes fifty million years to wear down the lunar surface by only one millimeter (.04 inches).

You, too, may be making a long-lasting impression.

TRIP #2. COPERNICUS CRATER

In 1919 an advertisement in the *New York Times* offered land on the Moon's Copernicus Crater for one dollar an acre. More than four thousand people sent money. They received a deed which promised "fishing and winter sports" on their property. A map sent with the deed enabled the moonstruck buyer to inspect his land through a telescope.

Although there's neither fishing nor winter sports, Copernicus Crater is so beautiful and unspoiled that it

has been declared an Interplanetary Park. No digging or building is permitted. It's even against the law to collect rocks in the park—a victory for nature-conservation groups.

The crater is named after Copernicus, the sixteenth-century astronomer who proved that planets revolve around the sun. Eight of our Grand Canyons can fit into it. The scenery has delicate pink and lovely lavender shades as well as white, gray, beige, and brown. Rimmed by walls two and three miles high, and holding a ten-mile mountain range in its bed, Copernicus is one of the Wonders of the Moon.

Even though several Moon craters are larger, travel folders tout Copernicus as "the Grand Canyon of Luna."

TRIP #3. THE LUNAR BADLANDS

Watch your step. The Badlands earned its name because the territory is pocked by tiny craterlets. It's dangerous to walk around alone. You must be leashed to two experienced guides who can pull you to safety if you fall in a crevice. Usually eight tourists are hooked to a rope that is attached to one guide who leads the way and one who brings up the rear. Tycho, Hell, and the Straight Wall are on the tour.

Tycho Crater, which is almost as big as Copernicus, is famous for its rays. The rays are streams of powdery soil that are lighter in color than most Moon soil. They streak out in all directions, crossing plains, mountains, valleys, and other craters. The rays splashed out when a meteorite crashed and formed Tycho millions of years ago.

You see the crater and its rays from the windows of your spaceplane before you land for a short stopover.

You'll have the thrill of seeing just where you were when you return home. You'll be able to look up at Tycho from Earth. It's the bright oval patch with white streaks on the lower left corner of the Moon. You can point up to it and say, "I was there."

After Tycho you go to Hell, a picturesque crater named after the seventeenth-century Jesuit astronomer, Father Maximilian Hell. Then, on to the Straight Wall inside the cloudless Sea of Clouds.

The Straight Wall is the only feature of its kind on the Moon. It's a steep cliff about eighty miles long and two miles high. Here's a perfect place to try Moon magic. Put your arm in the cliff's shadow. It looks as though it's been chopped off. Step into the shadow. You disappear. Shadows on the Moon are blacker than mine shafts because there's no air with dust particles to carry light into the shade.

TRIP #4. THE APENNINE MOUNTAINS

Fly into the right eye of the Man in the Moon: over the Sea of Clouds and across the Apennines to the Marsh of Decay Spaceport.

Rent a Moon buggy and follow the signs to Hadley Rill, a long, narrow valley surrounded by mountains. The rill is about a mile wide and sixty miles long. It was probably formed by lava flowing from a volcano.

Astronauts Jim Irwin and David Scott were here in 1971. They explored the area in the world's first Moon buggy, the Lunar Rover, and they planted an American flag at the base of Mount Hadley. You can stand next to it and have your picture taken.

TRIP #5. MOUNT LEIBNITZ

Climbing Mount Leibnitz is the goal of experienced mountain climbers. It's the highest mountain on the Moon, about a thousand feet higher than Mount Everest, Earth's highest peak (Mount Everest is 29,028 feet high).

Like all mountains on the Moon, Mount Leibnitz is smooth and round. Even though it doesn't have jagged cliffs and sharp peaks, and there's no ice or snow, you must be in top shape to reach the top. Should you become tired, no one can carry your oxygen backpack for you. You must have it to breathe!

When you reach the top, your guide will award you with a certificate which says that you have "conquered Mount Leibnitz."

The excursions mentioned thus far do not run during the two-week lunar night.

TRIP #6. THE FAR SIDE

The Far Side, also known as the Back Side, is the part of the Moon that does not face the Earth. It's as far away from home as a tourist can travel. And it's a complete rest for those who want to forget their roots, because there's no Earth in the sky to remind them of home.

Save this trip for the two-week night period on the Near Side. It will be day on the Far Side of the Moon.

During your trip around the Moon, you pass the "terminator," the "line" separating night from day. You feel as though someone has flipped a switch when you suddenly enter daylight from darkness.

Because the Soviets made the first map of the Far Side, most places have Russian names.

Take the Flying Troika from Moon Central Station to the Red Star Cosmoport on the Sea of Moscow. The

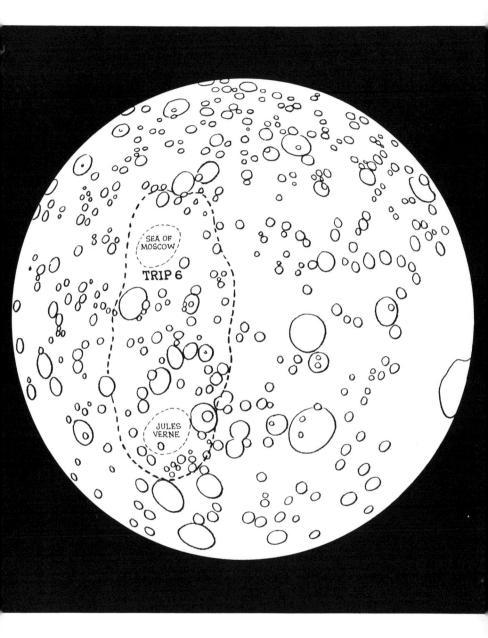

THE FAR SIDE

underground Lunagrad Hotel (★) has small but comfortable rooms and a good cafeteria-style dining hall. It is near two of the Far Side's unusual attractions: *Astronomer's Lookout* and the *Cosmos Listening Tower*.

ASTRONOMER'S LOOKOUT

The Moon is ideal for studying stars and planets. On Earth, astronomers have to look through an ocean of moving air that makes all objects in space waver and twinkle. Telescopes magnify this wavering effect.

Near-perfect images are seen through telescopes at Astronomer's Lookout. There's never any Earthglow, and the long, black nights are perfect for discovering new stars, planets, and asteroids.

Tourists are invited to peer through the largest telescope in the universe, made from glass and metal mined on the Moon. Here's your chance to take a good look at Mars, which should be ready for tourists by the year 2025.

THE COSMOS LISTENING TOWER

You won't hear a beep from Earth. Your radios and TV phones won't work because the Far Side is blocked off from Earth's sound waves by the Moon's two-thousand-mile thickness. Because there's no Earthly interference, scientists have set up a wide-dish radio antenna that is a mile round.

You see scientists from Cornell University and from the University of Vladivostok when you visit the Listening Tower. These scientists have been sending signals beyond our galaxy, hoping to be heard by intelligent creatures living in some way-out place in space, and they are listening for signals from them.

Anything is possible. Did you ever believe that you'd be walking on the Moon?

THE JULES VERNE REST HOME

Jules Verne was a French writer whose science-fiction novel *From Earth to the Moon* was published in 1865. His travelers were shot into space from a 900-foot cannon in Florida. When they came back to Earth, they splashed down in the ocean, like twentieth-century astronauts.

As a tribute to his genius, one of the Far Side craters is named after him. The Jules Verne Rest Home (½★), built in the crater in 1998, is for physically and emotionally tired Earthlings. It also attracts sad, silent, sullen types, moody mystics, and groups who practice TM (Transcendental Meditation). Guests sign up for a two-week stay.

A one-Earth-day excursion is possible. However, many tourists find the whole rest home scene depressing.

9

Moon Town

A fabulous village on the Near Side is within walking distance of your hotel. Moon Town was founded in 1990 by twelve American astronauts and twelve Soviet cosmonauts. According to the just-released "United Nations Census for the Year 2000," there are 4,752 residents in Moon Town, O.S. (Outer Space).

Walk or take a bus from the shopping arcade beneath your hotel.

Moon Town looks like a giant underground shopping center. Homes are on the west side of the town square. Shops and offices are on the east. The Medical Center and Hospital are on the north, and the Town Hall and Center for the Performing Arts are in the southern part of town.

Although Moon Town is inside a human-made cave far below the surface, it's brilliantly lighted by an artificial sun that rises and sets every twelve hours. It makes the rhythm of life more normal for Earthlings who immigrate to the Moon. Electricity comes from huge outdoor cells that collect and store solar energy.

Tourists always want to meet natives and learn about their habits and customs. However, most Moon dwellers guard their privacy. Only a few Moon Town homes are open for tourist inspection. Ask the Lunar Chamber of Commerce to arrange a visit.

When you are invited into a home, your host or hostess will undoubtedly ask you about conditions in the Old Country. You'll have a chance to ask them about their work and their life-styles.

Moon dwellers are proud to call themselves Lunarians. They are pioneers of our New World, immigrants who left planet Earth to start a new life in outer space. They are sensitive about some of the Earth humor aimed at them. If you want to be liked, don't call them "looneys." It's not funny. One well-known magazine had the bad taste to call them "bubbleheads" because they must wear round glass helmets when they leave town to go aboveground. Everyone does on the Moon!

Pioneer settlers of Moon Town are under forty years of age. Remember the excitement when the first Moon baby was born, on July 19, 1996? Newspapers all over the world announced the birth of Alpha 001. She weighed one pound four ounces (six pounds Earth weight) and was the bounciest baby ever born in the history of the universe. To date, there are forty-one baby Lunarians. Scientists wonder whether these children will ever be able to visit Earth. Will their bodies adjust to heavy gravity, temperature changes, germs, and impure air? How will they react to rain, snow, thunder, and lightning? Will insects and animals terrify them so that they feel that Earth is a planet for monsters? Time will tell.

Most adult Lunarians have full-time jobs. You see them working at hotels, parks, and science centers. You meet them on your excursions where they are your guides, pilots, and drivers. Many townsfolk commute to work in mines and in small factories. Newspapers constantly advertise job opportunities. There is no unemployment problem anywhere in outer space. Moon Town is a boom town. It is expected to double in size within two years. (Should you be interested in becoming a Lunarian, apply to the United Nations Department of Immigration.)

Tourists are not permitted in mines and factories. However, they are invited to see farmers at work.

THE HARVEST MOON FARM

Just a hop, skip and a jump from Moon Town (a quarter mile away) an underground greenhouse grows food for the Moon. Shafts of sunlight directed with mirrors are aimed at fifteen acres of plants.

Because the sun shines for three hundred sixty hours at a stretch, vegetables planted in the morning are ripe before dark. You see tomatoes the size of basketballs, and beans as big as baseball bats. They are grown from the latest miracle seeds.

Farmers don't have to worry about drought, frost, or floods. And there are no raiding insects, birds, or animals to ruin the harvest. Seeds are planted on plastic that has been treated with chemical fertilizers. Wheat and soybeans are the biggest crops.

Lunarians are vegetarians. The Town Fathers and

Mothers voted down a proposal for a pig farm and a chicken house. They refuse to import meat. Milk, cheese, eggs, nuts, and spices are sent from Earth to the Freight Depot once a week.

Hotel dining rooms are vegetarian, too. Moonburgers are made from carrots and soybeans. Vegetable chops, a mix of eggs, flour, mushrooms, and beans, are shaped and cooked to look and taste like beef. You'll enjoy the food. It's too bad the chefs refuse to give recipes.

10

Coming Down to Earth

You feel a slight jolt when Moonliner takes off from Moon Central Station. In the Moon's weak gravity, a spaceship uses only a fraction of the fuel it needs to take off from Earth.

After two days of floating and flitting in weightlessness, you transfer at Space Base to the shuttle.

During the last hour of the trip, flight attendants hand out rubber pantyhose. Go to the washroom and put them on. Use the rubber bulb attached to the pantyhose to pump air into them until they feel tight. This keeps blood from collecting in your legs when you come down to Earth.

Wear the pantyhose for two days after you've come home. You'll look fat, but you'll feel happy. While your body becomes used to our planet's pull, your mind can wander above the clouds, reliving memories of a heavenly holiday.

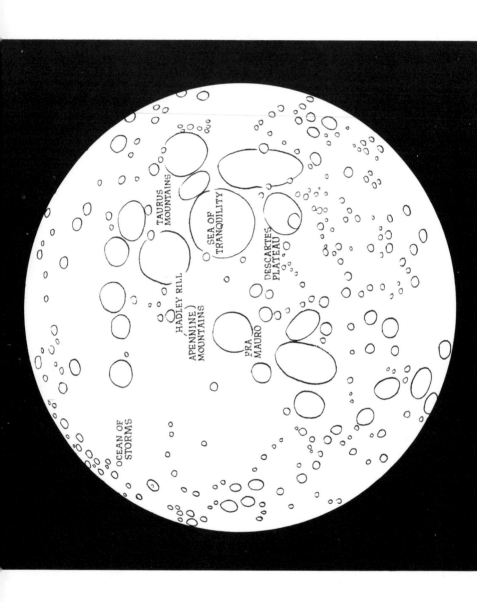

Our Pioneer Lunar Astronauts

ASTRONAUTS	LAUNCH DATE	LANDING SITE	MISSION
*Neil A. Armstrong *Edwin E. Aldrin, Jr. Michael Collins	July 16, 1969	Sea of Tranquility	Apollo 11
*Alan L. Bean *Charles P. Conrad, Jr. Richard F. Gordon, Jr.	November 14, 1969	Ocean of Storms	Apollo 12
*Alan B. Shepard, Jr. *Edgar D. Mitchell Stuart A. Roosa	January 31, 1971	Fra Mauro	Apollo 14
*David R. Scott *James B. Irwin Alfred M. Worden	July 26, 1971	Hadley Rill and Apennine Mountains	Apollo 15
*John W. Young *Charles M. Duke, Jr. Thomas K. Mattingly II	April 16, 1972	Descartes Plateau	Apollo 16
*Eugene A. Cernan *Harrison H. Schmitt Ronald E. Evans	December 7, 1972	Taurus Mountains	Apollo 17 (Last Apollo Mission)

*These astronauts landed and walked on the Moon.

Suggested Reading

Armstrong, Neil; Collins, Michael; and Aldrin, Edwin. *First on the Moon: The Astronauts' Own Story.* Boston: Little, Brown, 1970.
A first-class, first-hand account by the first men on the moon.

Clarke, Arthur C. *A Fall of Moondust.* New York: Signet Books, 1974.
————. *The Other Side of the Sky: Stories of the Future.* New York: Harcourt Brace Jovanovich, 1958.
A twentieth-century science fiction writer proves to be a gifted prophet.

Collins, Michael. *Flying to the Moon and Other Strange Places*. New York: Farrar, Straus & Giroux, 1976.
The pioneer astronaut's account of his training and his historic flight on Apollo 11.

Cooper, Henry S., Jr. *A House in Space*. New York: Holt, Rinehart & Winston, 1976.
How you feel in zero gravity, based on interviews with three Skylab astronauts.

DeNevi, Don. *To the Edges of the Universe: Space Exploration in the Twentieth Century*. Millbrae, Ca.: Celestial Arts, 1978.
The author anticipates a Moon town by the year 2000!

French, Bevin M. *The Moon Book*. New York: Penguin Books, 1977.
For readers interested in Moon geography and geology.

Glenn, Jerome, and Robinson, George S. *Space Trek: The Endless Migration*. Harrisburg, Pa.: Stackpole Books, 1978.
About mass migrations into outer space.

Heppenheimer, T.A. *Colonies in Space*. New York: Warner Books, 1978.
After your Moon journey, you should consider a vacation on a Space Colony.

Kahn, Herman. *The Next 200 Years*. New York: William Morrow, 1976.
Moon travel is seen in the author's crystal ball.

King, Henry. *Moon Rocks*. New York: Dial Press, 1970.
A rock collector's collector's item.

Lieber, Arnold L. *The Lunar Effect*. New York: Anchor Press, 1978.
Dr. Lieber claims that the Moon influences our moods and our actions.

Mailer, Norman. *Of a Fire on the Moon*. Boston: Little, Brown, 1971.
A lively account about the first astronauts on the Moon.

Moore, Patrick. *New Guide to the Moon*. New York: Norton, 1977.
The first detailed guide to that heavenly body we now know first-hand.

O'Neill, Gerard K. *The High Frontier: Human Colonies in Space*. New York: William Morrow, 1977.
The author, an acclaimed scientist who taught at Princeton, planned a city on an outer space satellite that could house 100,000 people.

82

Rush, Anne Kent. *Moon, Moon.* Berkeley, Ca.: Moon Books, 1976.
About ancient rituals, folklore, myths, and superstitions inspired by the Moon.

Verne, Jules. *From the Earth to the Moon.* New York: Dodd, Mead, 1959.
First published in 1865. Verne launched Americans to the Moon from Florida, not far from where the astronauts started their Moon journey a century later.

Wolfe, Tom. *The Right Stuff.* New York: Farrar, Straus & Giroux, 1979.
About the pioneer astronauts and their families, how they reacted to danger, and to fame no one had trained them for.